The Forensic Buddha

Solving Mysteries with Ancient Wisdom

Table of Contents

Chapter 1. Introduction

Dive into a thrilling convergence of ageless wisdom and cutting-edge science with our fascinating Special Report, "The Forensic Buddha: Solving Mysteries with Ancient Wisdom." This captivating journey isn't for the faint-hearted, as we venture behind the scenes of intricate crime-solving processes, but with a unique spin! Our experts reveal how they intertwine the tranquillity of Buddhist philosophy with the precision of forensic science to unlock mind-bending mysteries. Far from just technical case studies, this magical blend of science, spirituality, and detective work will keep you on the edge of your seat, eager to discover more. Don't miss an opportunity to acquire a fresh perspective on crime-solving, and maybe even instill some tranquillity in your own life along the way. Grab this Special Report today—let the mystery unravel and feel your curiosity ignite!

Chapter 2. Unveiling the Paradox: Ancient Wisdom Meets Modern Forensics

Modern forensic investigators stand on science's cutting edge, utilizing highly advanced techniques such as DNA analysis, trace evidence, digital forensics, and more. Yet, they contend with challenges that can hinder them from finding the truth — particularly dealing with the chaotic, tension-filled environments of crime scenes, which require a level of calm and focus that might sometimes be difficult to sustain.

2.1. The Serene Detective: Buddhism's Approach to Problem-Solving

Enter Buddhism, a philosophy developed over 2,600 years ago in the heart of ancient India—a time and place seemingly distant from our scientifically advanced, digital age. Founded by Siddhartha Gautama, known as the Buddha, it offers valuable lessons in tranquility, mindfulness, and living with intent.

While initially, it seems entirely unrelated to the raging world of crime-solving, a keen examination of Buddhist practices and teachings reveal underlying principles that bear remarkable correlation to the scientific method central to forensic investigation. They guide investigating a phenomenon objectively, testing hypotheses, and developing conclusions based on direct experience.

In particular, Buddhism promotes the idea of mindfulness, a state of concentrated awareness filled with caution, patience, and precision.

This concept prevails in a detective's meticulous combing for any signs or fragments left at a crime scene, demonstrating that following one's instinct does not mean abandoning evidence-based reasoning.

The Buddhist practice of 'Vipassana' or insight meditation fosters incredible clarity of thought and vision through introspection, somewhat similar to investigators' relentless probing in uncovering the truth hidden in minuscule details.

2.2. The Fusion: Synergizing Ancient and Modern Methods

Expounding on both worlds' coalescence, for instance, a team of forensics deals with a baffling cold case. The minimal evidence left behind and the forbidding wall of the case's vintage nature require more than just technical prowess. This situation entails equanimity, an unyielding focus and patience, traits learned and bolstered through Buddhist meditative practices.

Imagine a forensic scientist entering a room, staying mindful of their anxiety or fears, and remaining focused on systematically gathering data. They channel a Buddha-like tranquility amidst the chaos, focusing on the smallest details, undeterred by the harsh realities they witness.

In another instance, the principles of Karma—the law of cause and effect in Buddhism—help forensic practitioners to understand crime scenes. Everything at a crime scene is intrinsically linked, actions affect everything entwined in a vast web of connections, and forensic scientists bank on understanding this cosmic dance to decipher the past's secrets.

The significance of 'Pratītyasamutpāda' or dependent origination—a core concept in Buddhism—lies in comprehending the crime scene's complexity. Each element at a scene is interrelated and doesn't exist in isolation, charmingly similar to how every piece of evidence plays into the greater narrative of a crime.

2.3. Case in Point: Application of Bu-Forensics

Let's consider a hypothetical case—two bodies discovered in an old, run-down building, their identities and cause of death veiled in obscurity. Forensic experts find themselves contending with a chaotic crime scene: signs of struggle, a mix of different substances, and no clear story.

The lead investigator, trained in Buddhist techniques along with standard forensic procedures, builds a mental 'crime scene image'. They achieve a calm composure through mindfulness to accurse technology, connects each piece of the puzzle, preserving an open mind untarnished by prejudices or initial assumptions—that's the Buddha's way.

In another instance, consider the case of a string of thefts involving priceless artifacts. The traditional forensic path becomes elusive due to the stealthy perpetrator's modus operandi. Applying Buddhist principles, the investigation team slows down, invokes mindfulness, meditates on the crime scene, and meticulously scrutinizes every minute detail. Surprisingly, what appeared to be unrelated incidents show a pattern, further propelling their investigation.

2.4. Beyond Crime Scenes: Implications on Personal and Professional Growth

Beyond crime-solving applications, this harmonious merging of Buddhism and forensics poses significant potential for improving the forensic investigators' mental well-being.

Buddhist teachings insist that everything is transient, providing a stabilizing perspective to those dealing with heinous crimes' harsh realities, enabling them to handle their work without succumbing to overwhelming emotions. Furthermore, the practice of compassionate detachment helps investigators do their work without carrying the traumatic burden of crimes they explore.

It's fascinating, illuminating, and positively heartening to see how modern forensics and ancient Buddhist teachings come together in a symbiotic blend. Not only does each reaffirm the other's value, but they also create an engaging, enriching, harmonious method that can reshape our approach towards unravelling complex mysteries, ensuring justice, and even promoting personal growth.

As we move forward, striding into an increasingly uncertain future, it is perhaps wise to look back into the past. Wisdom does not always come dressed in the gown of new-age technology. Sometimes, it has the calm eyes and serene smile of a Buddha, and the precise eye of a forensic investigator.

Chapter 3. The Buddha's Path: A Primer on Buddhist Principles

Life can often be compared to a meandering journey over a mountain pass—steep, unpredictable, and full of various paths to navigate—each with its own set of hurdles and rewards. Buddhist philosophy, or the Buddha's Path, offers the traveller a compass, not telling them what to do, but providing frameworks to engage the world more effectively. It presents a sophisticated roadmap for ethical living, emotional health, and personal and societal liberation. The purpose of this text is to shed light on some of these fundamental Buddhist principles and how they may be employed in day to day lives.

3.1. The Four Noble Truths

Buddhist philosophy begins with what are known as the Four Noble Truths. First is the truth of suffering (Dukkha), the inherent dissatisfaction and unpredictability of life. However gloomy this may seem, it serves as a powerful reflection on the nature of existence, prompting individuals to strive for change.

Second is the truth of the origin of suffering (Samudāya), the cause of our dissatisfaction. It lies in our basic ignorance of the realities of life and the craving that arises as a result. Cravings—whether they be of sensory pleasures, survival, or eradication of what we dislike—bind us in a cycle of habitual and reactive patterns.

Thirdly, we have the truth of the cessation of suffering (Nirodha), a comforting implication that it's possible to interrupt these patterns.

Finally, comes the truth of the path to the cessation of suffering

(Magga), also known as the Eightfold Path. This comprises ethical conduct, mental discipline, and wisdom.

3.2. The Eightfold Path: A Roadmap to Liberation

The Eightfold Path offers concrete teachings to cultivate ethical behaviour, mental well-being and understanding.

Firstly, Right Understanding (Samma-ditthi) initiates the journey. It is the discernment of knowing things as they truly are, free from preconceptions or biases.

Right Thoughts (Samma-sanappa) follow, directing us to cultivate intentions of renunciation, goodwill and harmlessness, which counteract greed, ill-will and cruelty.

The third path, Right Speech (Samma-vaca), asks us to abstain from false speech, divisive speech, harsh speech, and idle chatter, reinforcing constructive communication.

The fourth aspect, Right Action (Samma-kammanta), encourages abstention from harmful deeds.

The fifth, Right Livelihood (Samma-ajiva), asks us to earn our bread without causing harm to others.

Next is Right Effort (Samma-vayama), guiding us in refraining from unwholesome states and in fostering wholesome states within.

The seventh, Right Mindfulness (Samma-sati), recommends constant awareness of the body, feelings, mind, and phenomena to prevent drifting into habitual patterns.

Finally, Right Concentration (Samma-samadhi)--the practice of meditative immersion, fostering clarity and perception.

3.3. The Middle Way

In the pursuit of spiritual liberation, the Buddha proposed the Middle Way. This philosophy avoids both the extreme of self-indulgence and the opposite extreme of self-mortification. It's a balanced approach to living – embracing neither luxury nor deprivation. The practice of insight meditation (Vipassana) is a practical implementation of such equilibrium.

3.4. Karma and Rebirth

Karma, a critical Buddhist concept, suggests a law of moral causation. Actions, driven by intention, lead to consequences. Conscious deeds craft our character, influence our destiny, and even affect our rebirth. The chains of cause and effect (Dependent Origination) mandate our cyclic existence (Samsara), and liberation (Nirvana) from this cycle is the ultimate Buddhist goal.

Here, the principle of rebirth emerges—not as a reincarnation where an eternal soul is reborn, but as a continuity of consciousness, evolving from one life to the next.

3.5. The Concept of No-Self

Lastly, the Buddhist concept of "No-Self" (Anatta) may challenge conventional views. Buddhism argues against the existence of an eternal, unchanging spirit or soul within us. Instead, it points out a stream of interconnected processes, with no independent or fixed entity to be found. Skilfully perceiving this notion can be liberating, quelling our egocentric tendencies and leading us towards compassion and kindness.

In conclusion, Buddhist principles aim to foster wisdom, ethical conduct, and concentration. Through the Four Noble Truths, the Eightfold Path, understanding Karma and rebirth, following the

Middle Way, and interpreting Anatta, these teachings offer timeless guidance for navigating life. Each concept intricately contributes to a comprehensive outlook towards individual and societal transformation.

Thus, the Buddha's path may unravel as a illuminating guide to living a more fulfilling life, if we are discerning and wise to follow it.

Chapter 4. Intricacies of the Crime Lab: A Forensic Overview

In a flurry of activity and controlled chaos, crime scene investigators and forensic experts create an orchestrated pandemonium, each maneuvering to fulfill their role. To an outsider looking in, this scene may appear overwhelming, but peel back the layers, and you'll discover a meticulous process exhibiting a juggling act of precision and efficacy.

4.1. Prerequisites of a Crime Lab

Let's begin with the critical prerequisites of a crime lab—investigative integrity and control. Investigators must observe defined policies and standard operating procedures, ensuring that evidence integrity is maintained throughout the process—from collection on the crime scene, during transportation, and even within the lab itself. These guidelines don't just apply to the tangible evidence, but extend to things like access control for personnel and site cleanliness so as not to introduce contaminants.

4.2. Forensic Disciplines and Departments

Forensic laboratories are often divided into several key departments, each dealing with a particular type of evidence. Often, these divisions include but are not limited to:

1. Biology/DNA

2. Fingerprint Analysis

3. Firearm and Toolmark Testing

4. Trace Evidence

5. Digital Forensics

6. Toxicology

Each department requires specific knowledge, tact, and equipment to handle the sensitive evidence.

4.3. DNA Analysis: Bare Bones of Identity

In the Biology/DNA department, technicians work to identify and quantify any biological evidence found at a crime scene. The extraction and purification of DNA from samples such as blood, saliva, or hair underscore the paramount importance of this process. The identification then often proceeds via techniques like Polymerase Chain Reaction (PCR), which replicates specific areas of the DNA helix many times over to facilitate analysis.

4.4. Beyond the Naked Eye: Fingerprint Analysis

Throughout the ages, mankind has understood that fingerprints are unique to each individual—a fact that has made it an indispensable tool in forensic science. In the realm of Fingerprint Analysis, experts delicately dust powders or chemical reagents onto surfaces to reveal unseen fingerprints, known as latent prints. These fingerprints can later be compared to a database or a specific suspect.

4.5. Silent Witnesses: Firearms and Tools

Objects we interact with often bear the imprint of our touch—visible and invisible marks that tell a story of their own. The Firearm/Toolmark Testing department engages in revealing those silent narratives. The unique rifling inside a firearm's barrel, or the precise cut of a tool, can often be matched directly to a weapon used, unearthing silent, inanimate witnesses of nefarious deeds.

4.6. A Speck of Truth: Trace Evidence

The smallest particle can sometimes reveal the greatest truths. Trace Evidence investigators, utilizing high-powered microscopes, spectral analysis, and a variety of other sophisticated techniques, analyze hair, fibers, paint chips, soils, glass fragments, and more, detailing their findings to construct a more circumstantial view of the crime event.

4.7. Charting the Digital Era: Digital Forensics

In the present digital age, a significant part of our lives is hedged into our devices. Information gleaned from smartphones, laptops, servers, and even vehicle infotainment systems can thus shed light on a crime's circumstances. Digital Forensics breathes life into this circuit-constrained, binary world, extracting essential data for use in investigations.

4.8. The Silent Protagonist: Toxicology

A crime isn't always committed with a knife or a gun. Sometimes, it's an unassuming drink or an innocent-looking pill. Toxicology enables the identification of drugs and poisons in body fluids, tissues, and even hair, silently testifying the invisible wounds inflicted.

Expertly maneuvering within these departments are the investigators and technicians. Their expertise collectively channels the orchestrated pandemonium, unveiling truths from beneath piles of evidence shard-by-shard, byte-by-byte.

4.9. Tools of the Trade

Now that we've examined the departmental intricacies of a crime lab, it's essential to spotlight the tools that assist these detectives in their investigations. Complex machinery like Gas Chromatography-Mass Spectrometry (GC-MS) allows for the separation and identification of complex mixtures, while devices like the comparison microscope perform side-by-side analysis of two samples.

Technology in forensic science has considerably evolved over time. Today, forensic labs harness Advanced Spectrometry Devices, 3D imaging, Biometric systems and Lab-on-a-chip technology to extend their analytical capabilities.

4.10. Bridging Ancient Wisdom with Modern Forensics

Interestingly, this convergence of cutting-edge technology and detailed procedural operations parallels Buddhist monastic life. The principles of mindfulness, awareness, meticulousness, and truth-seeking echo throughout the walls of both worlds—one of scientific inquiry and the other of spiritual discipline.

Yes, a crime lab might be chaotic, but beneath the seeming disarray, it is a place of incredible intricacy and precision, much like the mind entering a meditative state—a place where every particle, trace, and byte is carefully examined, and truth always sought.

As we've journeyed through the eclectic corners of a crime lab and glimpsed at its varied intricacies, we hope to continue fostering this sense of awakened inquiry, borne out of the fusion of age-old wisdom and modern forensics. Just like the lotus blooms amid the muck, may the truth always bloom amid the chaos. Never forget that even within the most sophisticated labs, the simplest wisdom can pave the road to truth.

Chapter 5. Clues in Calmness: Borrowing Serenity from Buddhism

The first rays of dawn were just peeking through the curtains of the case room when Special Agent Sarah Anderson walked in. She was known for her unflappable calm in the face of the most chilling crimes. Today's case, a mysterious homicide, was stunning in its complexity. But unknown to many, Sarah sought neither courage nor brilliance from the latest forensic gadgets or investigative techniques. Instead, she turned to a philosophy that was over 2,500 years old - Buddhism.

5.1. The Reservoir of Serenity in Forensic Investigations

Sarah knew the importance of maintaining a stable mind. Crime scenes are rife with chaos and distress. The sheer negativity they convey can overwhelm the sensors, distorting their perspective. It's crucial, then, for investigators to ground themselves, to stay balanced amidst the whirlwind.

This is where Buddhism comes in. An aspect central to Buddhist philosophy is mindfulness: the practice of being fully present and invested in one moment at a time. It teaches us to observe our thoughts and feelings without judgment. By adopting mindfulness, Sarah learned to objectively process the sights and sounds of a crime scene, without being gripped by the hysteria it often naturally conveys.

5.2. Mindfulness: A Precision Tool in Forensic Science

Investigating a crime scene is a meticulous process. Each small detail can hold significant clues. By staying present, Sarah often noticed minor inconsistencies that many missed in the urgency to solve the case. It's like each case was a giant jigsaw puzzle, and mindfulness allowed her to pick up the stray pieces lying just out of the immediate field of view.

Moreover, this unique blend of forensic science and mindfulness had far-reaching effects. By approaching each case without preconceptions, every piece of evidence was given due importance, and no potential lead was dismissed prematurely, which often is the pitfall of traditional crime investigation.

5.3. The Four Noble Truths: Frame for Crime Scene Analysis

Buddhism's Four Noble Truths, at their core, seek to understand the cause of suffering and ways to end it. Sarah found a unique application of this in her investigative work. The first noble truth, the Truth of Suffering, is recognizing that a crime has occurred. The second truth, the Cause of Suffering, is interpreting the crime scene evidence to understand why the crime occurred.

The third truth, the Cessation of Suffering, is piecing together the evidence to recreate the crime, and thereby determining how it can be prevented. Lastly, the Path leading to the Cessation of Suffering was implementing the prevention methods that will ideally keep others from suffering the same fate.

By structuring her investigations around the Four Noble Truths, Sarah promoted a methodical and all-encompassing approach to her work. Each section was given its due weightage, from recognizing and understanding the crime to preventing its recurrence.

5.4. Mastering the Art of Non-Attachment: Key for Objectivity

Sarah also embodied the Buddhist principle of non-attachment in her work. As forensic analysts, it's easy to get attached to initial theories or assumptions about the case. But such attachments can skew our perception and lead to cognitive biases that impede objectivity.

Non-attachment isn't indifference or aloofness, but rather the ability to let go of preformed notions to take in accurate observations. With this practice, Sarah ensured that she approached every new piece of evidence with openness and objectivity, thereby preventing faulty investigative decisions that could derail the case.

As forensic science continues to advance, the pressure on forensic professionals only escalifies. The methods, techniques, and technology improve, but so do the sophistication and cunning of criminals. However, by marrying cutting-edge forensics with age-old Buddhist wisdom, we can develop a more balanced, astute, and comprehensive approach to solve mysteries. We can, like Sarah, use tranquility as a tool, turning it from a passive state to an active investigative technique. That's the beauty of Buddhism—it offers a wellspring of serenity even in the most tumultuous circumstances, including the heart of a forensic crime scene. It truly is about finding clues in calmness.

Chapter 6. Buddhist Ethics in Forensics: The Impact on Crime Analysis

The application of Buddhist ethics and principles in forensic investigation offers a fresh perspective on analyzing criminal behaviour and seeking solutions to complex crime crises.

6.1. The Intersection of Buddha's Teachings and Forensic Science

Envision the core principles of Buddhism: the Four Noble Truths, the Eightfold Path, mindfulness, compassion, interconnectedness, and the pursuit of inner peace and enlightenment. Now imagine applying these teachings to the cutting-edge science of forensics, where every minutiae can form a fundamental piece of the crime-solving puzzle. To the uninitiated, Buddhism and forensics might seem like unlikely partners, yet many parallels exist between the two that can open new avenues for criminal analysis in forensic science.

Buddhist teachings revolve around understanding the inherent suffering of life, its causes, cessation, and the path leading to the cessation of suffering. When applied to crime analysis, these concepts encourage explorations into the roots of criminal activities in an effort to neutralize harmful behaviors. This initiative aligns with the idea of preventative crime measures that are focused on the basic causes of crime rather than their consequences.

Simultaneously, the Eightfold Path — right understanding, right intent, right speech, right action, right livelihood, right effort, right mindfulness, and right concentration — serves as an ethical compass guiding individuals away from destructive behaviors. Law enforcement professionals can use these teachings as a framework to view crime and justice differently, paving the way for innovative solutions in crime analysis and prevention.

6.2. Forensic Mindfulness: The Exploration of Psychological Traces

Crime scenes are not just about physical evidence; they bear psychological traces too. In this regard, Buddhist mindfulness practices can serve as an essential tool in forensic investigations. Mindfulness, as defined in Buddhism, is the conscious, non-judgmental focus on the present moment. It requires a high level of awareness and clarity, skills that are equally important in crime scene investigations.

In forensic psychology, insightful interviews and interrogations play a crucial role in piecing together crime narratives. A mindful approach can improve an investigator's ability to read subtle cues, enhance memory recall, encourage empathy towards victims, and conduct morally and ethically guided investigations. These methods not only augment the accuracy of crime analysis but also maintain the human approach required in delicate situations.

6.3. Unraveling Karma: Recognizing the Connectivity in Crime Analysis

In Buddhism, Karma isn't merely about cause and effect but also about interconnectedness. It tells us that our actions are like ripples on a water surface, influencing and being influenced by the environment around us. Applied to forensic science, this principle encourages investigators to acknowledge the wider ecosystem within which a crime operates.

This perspective facilitates multi-level crime analysis, linking individual actions to community dynamics, societal norms, or significant cultural influences. The understanding of the factors inter-knitted with offenses could help develop multidimensional, integrative criminal preventive measures and rehabilitation processes, ultimately promoting social reform and resilience.

6.4. Cultivating Compassion: Humanizing Crime Analysis Through Buddhism

Compassion lies at the heart of Buddhism's teachings. Criminal justice, where neutrality and objectivity ought to reign, can seem incompatible with compassion, viewed often as emotional bias. However, incorporating compassion doesn't hinder investigative processes or compromise objectivity. Instead, it serves as a reminder that criminal investigation involves human beings at its core.

A compassionate approach promotes balanced decisions, empathy with victims, and even non-hostile interactions with suspects, leading to more comprehensive and effective crime analyses. Importantly, this approach can positively impact prison rehabilitation programs, highlighting the significance of transformation and redemption over punishment.

The influence of Buddhist ethics in forensics and crime analysis extends far beyond these few aspects. Not only can these teachings enhance investigative precision and efficacy, but they also present an opportunity for restructuring criminal justice processes to be more humane, flexible, and driven by the intention of healing rather than punishment. This merger of Buddhism and forensic science offers a profound way to look beyond typical black-and-white narratives, acknowledging the complex spectrum of causes and effects that create the intricate tapestry of crime and justice.

Chapter 7. Meditation and Analysis: Cultivating Mindful Observations

The profound alignment of mindfulness meditation and forensic investigation may seem like an orthogonal association. However, when you delve deeper, you begin to unearth the extraordinary correlation between these two disparate elements. This cross-section offers a refreshing paradigm for the approach to crime solving, serving as a bridge between spiritual principles and scientific precision.

7.1. The Quintessence of Mindfulness

To understand how these two dimensions can intertwine, we must first understand the essence of mindfulness. Mindfulness, a core principle of Buddhist philosophy, refers to the ability to remain present, fully aware, and attentive of our physical experience, our actions, our emotions, and our thoughts, without our minds wandering to the past or the future. As we cultivate mindful observations, the clarity of our perceptions and understanding of reality gradually sharpen.

The practice of mindfulness meditation isn't just about establishing inner peace. In this state of heightened awareness, our discernment improves, allowing us to see discrete details often overlooked by the casual observer. These could be the subtle nuances in a conversation, or seemingly insignificant details in the environment—in a forensic setting, such observations could lead to breakthroughs in puzzling cases.

7.2. Principles for Analysis: From the Cushion to the Crime Scene

Applying mindfulness to forensics and investigations facilitates a novel way of perceiving scenarios. There are several ways this can manifest:

- Detached Observation: The skills honed in contemplative meditation—observation without emotional entanglement or prejudiced interpretation—can significantly enhance an investigator's ability to survey a crime scene objectively.

- Observed reality, not narrative: Practitioners of mindfulness develop the ability to stay deeply rooted in reality as it unfolds, refusing to get lured by hearsay, judgment, or preconceived ideas that could blur the objective interpretation of evidence.

- Patience and Diligence: In both meditation and forensic investigation, patience and diligence form the paradigm of advancement. Cases are not often resolved in swift, dramatic breakthroughs but through a rigorous series of smaller revelations patiently pieced together.

7.3. The Intersection of Mind and Matter: Neuroscience behind Mindfulness

Over the past two decades, neuroscience studies have found that mindfulness practice can literally reshape our brain. Neuroplasticity, the brain's ability to form new neural connections, enables significant changes in our cognitive and emotional responses. Long-term mindfulness practitioners show an enlarged prefrontal cortex—the area responsible for advanced cognitive processes like decision-making, attention, awareness, and empathy. This enhanced cognitive functionality complements the forensic analysis where detailed, impartial, and emotion-free observations are sacrosanct.

7.4. The Mindful Investigator: Real-life Applications of Buddhist Principles

As we have elucidated the theoretical framework of this integration, let us delve into real-life applications. Forensic experts attuned to mindfulness practice have used these principles to break ground in some of the most challenging investigations. They were able to keep their minds clear and composed in the midst of chaos, diligently studying the patterns, testing hypotheses, and eventually, penetrating the heart of previously unsolved mysteries.

7.5. Facets of Mindful Forensics: Training and Techniques

So, how do we apply the wisdom of the Buddha in the forensic world? Here are some starting points:

1. Mindful Observation: This starts with training the senses to be present and absorbent of details, no matter how minute. The observation of breathing and bodily sensations during meditation hones this ability.

2. Sustained Focus: A vital part of meditation is the art of grounding the mind and avoiding distractions—an essential skill for an investigator spending hours analyzing files and evidence.

3. Emotional Equanimity: Mindfulness practitioners learn to calm their minds and regulate their emotional responses – a skill of immense value in maintaining one's composure in stressful situations arising during crime-solving.

These principles represent the tip of the iceberg. With focused training and practice, mindfulness meditation can be turned into a potent tool in the hands of crime investigators, aiding them in their quest for justice.

In conclusion, the convergence of ageless wisdom in the form of mindfulness meditation and cutting-edge forensic science can lead to a revolution in criminology. Through a balanced application of these principles, we stand at the precipice of a fascinating journey—one that is at once profoundly spiritual and scientifically rigorous. But the journey begins with the ignition of individual mindful curiosity. We encourage you to take the first step, observe, engage, and see beyond the obvious. After all, an enlightened mind is the most powerful detective.

Chapter 8. Unraveling Complexity: Solving Cases with Buddhist Simplicity

At the intersection of mindfulness and advanced forensics, our story begins. Traditionally, crime-solving methodologies have been solely analytical, rooted in the evidentiary findings, logic, reasoning, and detailed examination. But what happens when we turn to an ancient philosophy, Buddhism, to simplify and pacify the byzantine maze of clues that surround a case?

8.1. The Marriage of Buddhism and Forensic Science

Buddhism, a philosophy advocating for mindfulness and awareness, provides an intriguing complement to the empirical rigor of forensic science. The fusion is surprisingly profound, uniting the tranquility of the former with the precise, methodical nature of the latter. It can be argued that the secret to successful crime-solving may lie in the integration of these seemingly divergent realms.

Mindfulness, the cornerstone of Buddhist practice, emphasizes the importance of being present and taking a moment-by-moment approach to life. This philosophy is incorporated into the investigative process to create an environment that nurtures patient observation, careful detailing, and comprehensive analysis. When combined with scientific forensics, this philosophy encourages investigators to anticipate unexpected connections, enhance their decision-making skills, and widen their scope of understanding.

8.2. The Art of Mindful Investigation

The first principle of embedding Buddhism into the investigative process lies in the adoption of mindful observation. Instilling attentiveness at the scene of the crime, detectives are trained to inhale the sights, sounds, smells, and atmosphere to form a holistic context before embarking on the scientific part of the investigation.

This mindful immersion allows them to create mental maps of the scene, which helps later during evidence analysis. It encourages them to pick up on minute details that could aid the investigation and adjust their perspectives to view the event from multiple standpoints.

8.3. A Journey into the Self

In parallel with their work on the cases, the investigators also embark on an inward journey. By practicing meditation, they learn to cleanse their mind of biases, preconceived notions, and judgment patterns that tend to cloud objective analysis. In essence, they work towards creating an unbiased mind, a crucial tool that helps them decipher the trails and deception often left behind by criminals.

Equipped with a quiet mind, forensic detectives are able to approach each piece of evidence with fresh eyes, bringing an element of intuition coupled with logic to the process. The end result is often an insightful, layered, and thoughtful analysis that has the potential to shed new light on even the most convoluted of cases.

8.4. Emphasizing Compassion and Understanding

A key principle of Buddhism is compassion and understanding, even towards those who have committed wrongdoings. This notion resonates in the world of crime-solving too. While it does not excuse the criminal's actions, it influences detectives to explore the motive behind the crime and the circumstances that led up to it.

Developing empathy helps investigators understand the drives and triggers of suspects, enabling them to formulate connections and patterns they may have otherwise overlooked. It bridges the gap between the evidence and the human circumstance, which is key to painting the complete picture of the crime scene.

In conclusion, the utilization of Buddhist principles in forensic science provides an all-encompassing approach to solving mysteries. It creates a unique environment in which the unfettered tranquility of Buddhism mingles with the rigorous logic and scientific aptitude of forensics in the quest to uncover truths. This philosophy doesn't just hold promise for crime-solving, but it also challenges all of us to think differently, to adopt mindfulness in our lives and to see the world through a more empathetic and discerning lens.

8.5. The Way Forward

This convergence between ageless wisdom and cutting-edge science promises a paradigm shift in crime investigation approaches. The melding of the inner tranquility of Buddhism and the advanced techniques of forensic science perhaps suggests a new era of understanding and solving crime.

It underscores the potential that lies within this hybrid approach, propelling investigators into a future where they not only solve crimes but also reach a state of inner peace and clarity. The path to the truth, it seems, might just lie as much within us as it does in the evidence collected at the crime scene.

The opportunity this presents - for detectives, for science, and for our society - is thrilling. As more investigators and scientists embark on this path, unlocking mysteries with the tranquillity of Buddhism and the precision of forensic science, this approach may redefine our understanding of the concept of problem-solving itself.

And meanwhile, as we journey through our lives alongside them, maybe, just maybe, we too can learn to apply these principles to navigate our personal mazes and unravel our own complexities. For in the end, aren't we all detectives, seeking answers, using tools at our disposal to understand and navigate the intricacies of life's endless mysteries?

Chapter 9. Profound Parallels: Buddhists' Right View and Forensic Objectivity

In the awakening depths of Buddhist philosophy lies a key tenet, labeled as 'Samma-Ditthi' or rightly known as the 'Right View.' On the other side of the spectrum is the realm of forensic science, where objectivity holds a pedestal, acting as a cornerstone for every ensuing investigation. And, you might ask, where is the connection? The parallels lie in their core functioning principles, though appearing divergent in their applications.

"In seeing, there is just seeing. No seer and nothing seen. In hearing, there is just hearing. No hearer and nothing heard," Buddha illuminated this 2600 years ago. When investigators embrace forensic science, this axiom becomes an employer of clarity in observations, curbing personal biases, and removing any preconceived notions about what they 'should' find.

9.1. The Prism of Right View

The 'Right view' as per Buddhist teachings emerges as an all-encompassing perspective that encourages perceiving things as they are, unclouded by personal experiences, biases or expectations. Buddha posited that Samsara (the cycle of death and rebirth) binds us, and inherent in life is suffering. To liberate from this ceaseless wheel of existence, understanding the Four Noble Truths is fundamental.

1. Dukkha: The truth of suffering

2. Samudaya: The truth of the origin of suffering

3. Nirodha: The truth of nirvana, cessation of suffering

4. Magga: The truth of the path to the cessation of suffering

These beliefs indoctrinate seeing realities in their truest essence, void of subjective coloring and distortions. Living by 'Right View' is akin to illuminating darkness, revealing what was concealed under the sway of ignorance or bias.

9.2. Forensic Objectivity: A Beacon in Uncertainty

As scientists take a plunge into the sometimes murky waters of criminal investigations, objectivity becomes their anchor. Believe none of what you hear and half of what you see—forensics thrives on this axiom. While 'forensics' inherently means 'the forum,' owing its origin to Roman times when criminal charges were debated in public, modern forensics has refined its role into an unbiased seeker of truth.

The scientific method is the pillar of forensic science, combining rigorous empiricism and relentless skepticism. It begins with observations that stir questions, leading to hypotheses and carrying out experiments to gather evidence, which is then analyzed to reach conclusions. The findings' validity lies in their reproducibility, irrespective of who conducts the experiment or investigation; hence, the emphasis on objectivity.

9.3. Transecting Parallels: The Intersection Point

Seemingly disparate, these two spheres of knowledge converge in their pursuit to see things "as they are." While Buddha taught the 'Right View' to alleviate suffering and lead to Nirvana, forensic science utilizes objectivity to abstract truth from clues left behind at a crime scene.

Forensic practitioners embody the Buddhist principle of 'Right View' as they set aside personal biases, conducting investigations propelled only by where the evidence leads. They focus on the task without being swayed by their personal beliefs, attitudes, or emotions—a task easier said than done.

Consider two detectives at a crime scene following a violent conflict. One inspector observes the scene and immediately, unconsciously associates it with a particularly gruesome case he had dealt with before. This unconscious correlation may cloud his judgement, biasing his interpretation of the evidence. However, the other investigator, trained to embody elements of the 'Right View,' works methodically through the scene, laser-focused on logging the evidence. Her investigations and conclusions are based solely on the evidence before her, with no influence from past experiences.

9.4. Implementing the Right View in Forensics

Adapting the 'Right View' in forensic science is no easy feat, given human tendency towards biases. Buddhism, through mindful meditation and conscious efforts, puts forth methods to attain the 'Right View.' Forensic professionals can inculcate similar meditative practices, fostering mindfulness, aiding in being fully present at the moment, and focusing on the task at hand. Evidently, when unwavering focus and attention to detail merge, the outcome rings with truthfulness and accuracy. Cultivating the 'Right View' in forensic settings embarks a path to unwavering observations and analyses.

Indeed, the 'Right View's' principles pave the way for bias-free observations. This applies not only to crime scene investigations but also in lab analyses, suspect identification, and interpreting the evidence. It is an investment in mental clarity and impartiality that yields transformative results.

9.5. The Rewards of Convergence

Buddhist wisdom and modern forensic science seemingly exist in two different realms. One deals with the inner world, and the other scrutinizes the tangible, physical world. However, the convergence of these two—inspired by the common principle of seeing things 'as they are'—brings forth a fresh lens, a novel bedrock for forensic practitioners, enhancing the effectiveness of their investigative procedures, thus bringing them closer to the truth.

This magnificent blend of spirituality's profound wisdom and forensic science's sharp precision holds the promise for better outcomes in criminal investigations, all the while, possibly bringing about a peaceful equilibrium in practitioners' personal lives. The fusion of ancient wisdom and cutting-edge science is indeed a mesmerizing dance of paradoxes—the convergence delightful yet profound, challenging yet rewarding.

As we explore further, are there more such intersections in store? Only time and deeper exploration will tell. After all, investigations, much like the journey to enlightenment, are matters of relentless questioning and ceaseless seeking.

Chapter 10. Victimology from a Buddhist Perspective: Compassion Amidst Chaos

In the heart of Buddhism lies the principle of compassion—an understanding of others' suffering and a desire to alleviate it. This foundation on empathy provides a unique lens through which to view victimology—the study of crime victims, their relationships with offenders, and their interaction with the criminal justice system. It is through this compassionate lens that Buddhism enriches victimology, driving a deeper understanding of victims' experiences which, in turn, aids investigations and promotes justice.

This chapter will unfold the depths of this thought-provoking convergence, creating an expanded viewpoint on the complex world of victimology.

10.1. The Concept of Compassion in Buddhism

The Buddhist ethic of compassion, known as 'karuṇā', isn't merely a feeling but an active quality, stirring a readiness to address and relieve suffering wherever it arises. This particular notion of attuned empathy allows a more profound understanding of victims' experiences.

For instance, the 'Brahma Viharas' or divine dwellings—the Four Immeasurables— consist of compassion, sympathetic joy, equanimity, and loving-kindness, and serve as guidelines on how to interact empathetically with others. By employing these teachings when interacting with victims, one can build a sturdy bridge of trust and openness, thereby gaining access to critical details for investigation unseen from a literal perspective.

10.2. Victimology from a Buddhist Compassionate Lens

To apply 'karu□ā' in the realm of victimology means empathizing with victims without losing sight of the primary objective: to solve the crime. It involves understanding victims' experiences and reactions in the backdrop of their individual circumstances and the crime context.

Victims may encounter trauma, fear, or shame in the aftermath of a crime. By approaching these experiences with a compassionate orientation, investigators can ensure victims feel seen, heard, and respected. Moreover, creating a 'safe space' promotes transparency, which is key to uncovering essential details of the crime.

10.3. The Path to Understanding Suffering: The Four Noble Truths

The Four Noble Truths in Buddhism sketch the nature of suffering ('dukkha'), its origin, the possibility of its cessation, and the path leading to its cessation. Through the lens of victimology, the Four Noble Truths can serve as a guide to understanding victims' experiences and their response to trauma.

The First Noble Truth, acknowledging suffering, involves recognizing the victim's pain. The Second Noble Truth, understanding the origin of suffering, provides insight into the victim-offender relationship. The Third Noble Truth, centred on the cessation of suffering, highlights the need for justice and closure. The Fourth Noble Truth signifies the journey towards that closure, which is facilitated by the investigation and eventual trial.

10.4. The Five Precepts and Victim-Offender Relationship

The Five Moral Precepts in Buddhism represent a code of personal conduct, serving as determinants of karmic reactions. Unraveling these precepts aids the examination of the victim-offender relationship.

The violation of one or more precepts could potentially explain the motive or mindset behind an offender's actions and affect the victim's reactions. Mapping this out with reference to the five precepts provides an innovative tool for profiling the offender, hence an edge in the investigation.

10.5. Balancing Compassion with Equanimity

Equanimity ('upekkhā'), one of the Four Immeasurables, is key to ensuring a compassionate approach doesn't compromise objectivity. Without a balanced state of mind, an overflow of empathy could cloud judgement or create bias. Therefore, the cultivation of equanimity is crucial for any investigator applying Buddhist principles.

10.6. Using Mindfulness to Enhance Victim Interviews

Mindfulness—or full present-moment awareness—can be utilized effectually within victim interviews. It ensures careful attention to the victim's words, behaviour, and emotions, potentially leading to unnoticed insights. It also encourages a calm, non-judgmental approach, emphasizing active listening rather than preconceived notions.

10.7. From Victimology to 'Ripples of Impact'

Traditionally, victimology focuses on the immediate victim. But the Buddhist focus on interconnectedness expands this range, taking into account the 'Ripples of Impact'—considering family members, friends, and the community affected by the crime. This broadened view can help map the wider impact and fallout of the event, hence providing a more holistic understanding of the crime's implications.

10.8. The Significance of Closure from a Buddhist Perspective

The concept of closure is important in Buddhism, in terms of victims finally attaining peace and moving away from suffering. The final action, therefore, is to ensure victims are afforded closure, whether that means taking perpetrators to justice or helping victims seek professional mental healthcare.

In conclusion, Buddhism's insightful teachings can be seamlessly woven into the field of victimology, offering a fresh, compassionate perspective on understanding victims and solving crimes. Not only does this convergence promotes better investigations, but it also fosters a nurturing environment for victims, facilitating healing and closure.

Chapter 11. The Forensic Buddha: Case Studies in Enlightenment and Detection

In the heart of every mystery, there's a whisper of truth waiting to be heard. Our inaugural journey into the realm of "The Forensic Buddha" takes us on an exploration of fascinating cases that would be impenetrable enigmas without the fusion of ancient wisdom and cutting-edge science.

11.1. The Case of the Silent Oracle

Lucas Hardy, a seasoned detective, had been engaged in a 48-hour deadlock with a murder case when he decided to take a remarkable approach. Inspired by his personal interest in Buddhist teachings, he started his investigation by meditating, hoping to find some illumination there. His quest was to piece together a fragmented narrative: a theft that led to murder, and the only clue left at the crime scene—a statue of the laughing Buddha.

The stolen object was a precious heirloom—an antique necklace of unparalleled and insurmountable worth. Witnesses described an ominous figure fleeing the scene but could not provide enough detail to assist in crafting a composite sketch. The victim, having lived a life of solitude, had no known enemies, yet met with such violence. None of it made sense.

Lucas sought the tranquillity necessary to delve deeper into the mystery, employing Buddhist principles of mindfulness and deeper seeing to do so. Scrutinizing the Buddha statue, he observed its cheerful countenance, reflecting on the contradiction it presented amidst the gruesome reality.

Ironically, tranquillity was indeed found in the silent laughter of the Buddha statue. Upon closer inspection, Lucas discovered hidden compartments—one in the belly, the other in the base. The former held traces of an ancient seal; the latter, residual dust. Quantitative element analysis of the dust identified several rare minerals, pointing to a specific island in the South Pacific.

The seal, weathered by time, had resemblance to the symbols native to the same topography. Investigations led the team to an illegal artefact smuggler operation on the island. The connection between the theft, the murder, and the Buddha statue was now clear. The heirloom necklace and the statue had been part of the valuable fenced articles.

Lucas's blend of Buddhist serenity and scientific precision had not only shed light on a seemingly unsolvable mystery but was also instrumental in dismantling an international smuggling ring.

11.2. The Shadow of Distorted Karma

In the heart of downtown, a series of incidents had left the local community in fear. Victims found with peculiar physical injuries hinted at a serial offender. Detective Sandra Shaw, an ardent practitioner of Buddhist principles, took the lead on the case.

Puzzled by the recurring pattern of injuries found on the victims, she infused her deductive processes with the Buddhist concept of karma—the action and reaction cycle. Sandra postulated a correlation between the victims' actions and the subsequent inflicted injuries but needed evidence.

Forensic examination of the crime scenes revealed trinkets subtly placed, each alluding to Buddha's Eightfold Path. The criminal, it seemed, was exercising a warped form of justice, using the principles of karmic retribution to justify their heinous actions.

With this understanding, Sandra meticulously unraveled the connections between each victim, discovering that they were all implicated in various morally questionable activities. Guided by this new lead, evidence soon pointed towards a specific individual with undeniable resentment against the victims and a distorted understanding of Buddhist karmic philosophy.

The convergence of Buddhism and forensic science had led to another breakthrough. It not only provided a solution for the case but exposed the dangers of manipulated spiritual understanding, particularly the incorrect interpretation of karma.

11.3. Enigma Hidden Within Zen Gardens

The serene beauty of Zen gardens often exudes a sense of peace and tranquility. Yet, they abruptly turned into crime stages, with unidentified remnants of human remains appearing mysteriously among the meticulously cared-for rocks and sand.

Detective Adrian Douglas, profoundly influenced by Zen Buddhism, saw a potential answer residing within this very art of delicate balance and symmetrical aesthetics. Zazen—the Zen Buddhism meditation practice became his guide.

Endowed with an intimate understanding of Zen aesthetics, Adrian noticed peculiarities in the garden arrangements. As a result, he was able to identify a secret cipher hidden within the seemingly random arrangement of rocks and vegetation.

Utilizing this cipher and correlating it with forensic evidence – the age and origin of the bone fragments, he discovered connections between the victims and a criminally inclined religious cult. The cult, under the guise of promoting Zen principles, practiced human sacrifices to attain a perverse form of enlightenment.

Both the peaceful pagoda and the forensic lab were integral to Adrian's deduction. The insights drawn from Zen balanced the cold precision of forensics, leading him to uncover the dreadful secrets these tranquil gardens held.

Each case reveals the extent to which Buddhist wisdom and serenity could blend with forensic science, highlighting the interconnectedness so sought after in Buddhism. As we synchronously connect mindfulness with scientific precision in our quest for truth, we discover new layers to both realms. We'll probe further into more heart-wrenching enigmas in the upcoming chapter, shedding light on the hidden tales concealed in the silence of unsolved mysteries.